Ian Davidson

Also by Ian Davidson:

It Is Now As It Was Then (with John Muckle),
Actual Size, London, 1983
No Passage Landward, Open Township, Hebden Bridge, 1989
Human to Begin With, Poetical Histories, Cambridge, 1991
The Patrick Poems, Amra Imprint, London, 1991
Wipe Out, Short Run, Cheltenham, 1995
Human Remains & Sudden Movements,
West House Books, Sheffield, 2003.
Harsh, Spectacular Diseases, Peterborough, 2003.

At a Stretch

Ian Davidson

Shearsman Books
2004

First published in the United Kingdom in 2004 by
Shearsman Books
58 Velwell Road
Exeter EX4 4LD

http://www.shearsman.com/

ISBN 0-907562-44-2

Acknowledgements

Some of these poems have previously appeared in the following magazines, often in earlier versions.

Chicago Review, A Chides Alphabet, The Gig, GutCult, Masthead.

The author wishes to thank the editors for their support.

CONTENTS

The Keokuk Poems

Keokuk

from each contact point diagrams open out
like Waltons walk carpeted hallways from
deplaning so dry a landscape so sure the
sun my memory stores a sign

within link corridors without a prayer the
conveyor stops on taxi an exceptionally
dry face some turbulence lower altitude
I mean attitude the turbines keeping faith

hair travel

lines of rivers mountains frozen over lake
suspended between places the rain in
local time away the talk soft

I am within mist
I am far away
I is evergreen

ground force

beyond light
cloud sunshine

within darkness a mass
treaty with gravity

beneath the airwaves the breadth of
band along the ground that is the
map traverse vapours break up

English is the language of thieves
the sun coming at it slant
everything they say or do squalls
shuttle to and fro upon the wing

and air off and warped above
the structures of the sky
deciding what does 'something'
do its absence death or other

films decline their
declension a letting go
the incomplete context white
clouds feeding into snow

poem

I photographed the bald eagle

I showered and shaved

like the tv only colder
I
constructed pathways
a
map becomes a diagram

religious building

at the temple a pile of vague
references on consecration they
rip out the soft furnishings

authenticity has a low shadow
the woman who drowned her children
speaks to camera a ring
of bulls sing for supper he
unscrewed his ears the sound
can take you far away working
within distance every day I drank

terrestrial

looking up to the moon and stars

tellestrial

parking in the sea of moon into

celestial

as heavenly as it is

almost too much
the rotting trees along the riverbank
an action of following the curves
the hatched granite series of
moons facing the sky
the dead centre sun that cannot hold

Cedar Springs

we followed the power lines north
across the money by pass
a small sigh of disappointment
her protection behaving badly
many channels of misinformation
little left over walked
wrote about it

Quincy

All over the place
I am all and over my

Enough ground elder
Beyond the state baptise

Dead people absorption all
Chicken stripped out

Every device roped
Light and grassed flat

Ready beyond greed
Falling sleepy beef

Range

Within the travel to
warmth area
spurred by the
need to express myself
tiny fingers
hooked in the
blanket what eyes
have or the shiny rail
all ears pointing
direction of
sound envelope of
heat when
in the comfort zone
of impossibility
like the cake walk

Michael

A day's ride across the hot plate
dishes pass or dangling children
from the balcony words drip like
collagen from his lips he's
a consequential an opening left
by another's disappearance
being beaten back or within
range as if the body won't work

Hospital

Uninformed pretty consistently clothes
are normally dehydrated or
dead on the roof top speckled
air voices as if from a great
distance screwing the jaw
into alignment lining the bite back
into the small shattered pieces of
bone old European war war
new nerve endings unravelled
inspection ratings up oil stocks down

the commercial strip

across crowded rooms within
whatever cost code
they talked until the last minute
scrubbed rows of beach facing seaward
through cloud cover this is America

I take an interest as a percentage
concentrate go for a walk
an industry only ever sustains itself
that's its business

her hair fell across her face
he lifts his arm
oh distant star for listening your soft
obscenity beyond language
I balloon
sorry I ever started
borne by many hands
he looked around his
cruise control gone
all hands on deck

someone standing at the queue more
tinned beans beyond the sell by date
like truth by Klein more fries no
wings I flies the Keokuk poems

Buffer Zone

in density

1.

when there's money or people
in the question to dispense and
still hanging around or mad
through the window

pale figure sits looks out
figure alone sits his money gone
to the four winds money gone
west and now what

the brains of 20,000 mad
people or at least certified their
relative sanity in uproar within
the circular sore fragments of
bone in the brain

water does flow uphill
I know this now I've rafted I've canoed
there are no firm foundations when shifting class
the things that might be base; metal, music
chairs become chains, metal mental
better than
thought
suspended in a state of indecision
between 99 and the full pound
desolate influence shades of trees

2.

they were young and their Moldavian first class

they slept in cinemas through the afternoon

Yes sir between the documentary and the film there is an interval which is not too expensive

temporary structures swayed around their heads
arranged to collapse inwards and conceal the bodies
in case of accident

free of any reference points
they captured the precise mood

All	The	Way
Free	To	Roam
Fail	Safe	Device
Prince	Of	Peace
For	Love's	Gracious
Hand	To	Mouth
Shut	Da	Fuck
Of	Great	Courage
Go	Back	Home

3.

at the end of the valley
a lake where grounds
finally settle toxins
take up residence

the only evidence
a handful of receipts
in the empty plazas
where people lived

each gesture familiar vendors
knowing their place each
temporary structure someone and son

dashed to death and
awful stuck
voices I really
don't know
the ethics of asking questions
of the poor like what's it like
being poor

4.

lessons in abstraction

a big fat zero

a mask of nerve tissue

sailing the ship of capital
foaming at the mouth
until love redeems me

O Xena in your uncanny way
reveal to me my manor

5.

SEA TUNNEL CLIFF MIST

boy zone

family zone

experimental garden zone
biological warfare

as smooth as milk and safer
documents rolled up tight
against the sale of good land

SAMPLING NOW

diving down and re-emerging
with a brick like chicken skin
or the marbled fat of lamb

BOYZ TO MEN

review long walks thinking
personal injuries theory
water culture the Life of Riley

RADIOACTIVE SEA AND SAND

I saw your flat white stomach
and as I poured another glass
I thought this is a mistake and then the news showed
a crowd chasing paedophiles through
the street and signs saying go back home but
that seems the last place they can go to

UP MY ALLEY

I read something and thought it was by someone else
I put words in their mouth
packing out the fillings
smoothing down the sharp edges
and then I had to turn them on their head
and shake so the words fell out

I shuffled back to lean on the bark of the tree

you get a lead and then follow it to the bitter end

the photocopied head of concrete poetry
she went all armadillo put her shields up
her weapons more than those on open display

6.

the way hot a child moaned on a man's arm
no feel for language or separation by time
the presence of running water but up close
and impenetrable to the public gaze
the crazed surface of miniature landscapes
inherited arm movements
a slight inclination ash falls

plant life

1.

sand at so much a layer
the foot rested near the head
it's a position
the face sucked in
straightened out
its feet outside the curtilage

the site inverted
monument beaten flat and
wrapped around the globe
from forests tumours eyes
bore holes in the ice, fished out
bruised from all that seeing

in sky and light
in density I camp out wound
down the sedimentary canal along
the towpath I cast in
as far as the I can see
to the socket's extent

shutting down the body parts
plugging in the body parts
exit to port
entering port
sand filled the eye socket
recently disturbed

2.

It was Paris 1975 and my elbow formed the fulcrum around which his forearm might pivot. She was skittish – alone and disturbed – the bust of JFK – while in the square in Galway town tablets of text emerged. Beneath the feet of great men through the whites of her eyes to Martello tower. She was donated to the state for the benefit of the nation. She took to the needle. She got to the hump.

3.

reading the legend
we took the commercial strip
in a bare landscape
look at flora bypass
the consensus

the statutes of Kilkenny
no inter-breeding with the English
my single strand of blonde
across the attention span of autism
everything, day and night,

it was bog standard
a plantation house
its function to become

there is little possibility of finding the best means of
gaining entry across loose ground
figure it out
I take the original and crack it like a chestnut
singing and dancing, religious questions

gasping he turned right a figure of
ate the English reel sentiment
simply suppression of difference

4.

in tent city the rain never stopped

the north wound up their windows

following a process of implantation the people
grew genetically frail my exploration of their
frozen culture took some time I took the long
way round got in through the back pulling
down the shades it was a premiere site

I couldn't keep up the pace
mass eviction behind
the lines and because of
desertion they set up the cells

bees moved back and forth

positioned across the saddle with both
feet on the floor I felt the ground tremble
my mosquito net full to the brim
his anger management

5.

lens go pixellate barely awake
I cannot foresee scattered
boulder matter
where the air came from
hoping for some improvement
behind the fly wire keeping
the exits clear beyond the pale

6.

it was nightly
against the dark sky figure becomes ground
I associate with maps
monsoon weather
landscape
no escape
every day a different island
accustomed to humans
to the steady chop of deforestation
and all I can do is repeat
across the road etc
to the river etc
between the flags of Ulster
on the banks of Mourne
a belief in new poverty
framed by the river they
work in arch enemies
as the money passed me by
the river curved him around

7.

I walked I was flagged down
caught red handed Ulster
is a mist before the eyes
air between the upper limits
registered roads unclassified
byways to go
the money to stay

he phoned home but
his number was up

8.

from O'Che's place deep in the
Galway jungle dogs bark
rolling out the lines of a lifetime

I asked again – how are you
she turned her head away and looked down
she ran her fingers across the table
she plucked at the spot on her chin

let's talk about hair

sodden movements

9.

caught red handed
biting to the nail
little conversation
from the peace dividend
I roll back the eyes
lift the lids, ferret
it was a cool way to be
bare above the knees

across the divide
into enemy territory
as if everything is ok
in my dry phase
when the rain came
the eating phase
brown autumn began to turn
my hands to myself
people do believe in the system
syntax all over the place

I swallow nervously cling to a wire
ripe fruits appear clustered at the branch end
closure is inorganic

10.

across the excavated beds sand drifts
each excavated grain
returns and turned again

cut a cross section
articulated layers
speak volumes
the date of ploughing
the way turf is turned

from the details pictures
from the fragments of bone bodies
it was how it was meant to be

this is not a state of the art
simply sand moving between its selves and
these procedures the bucket and spade
flash of the digital camera

why should it have been any way else
how could it have been any place else

11.

from the 7th century her hair remained swept
across her right shoulder and blonde

she got the alarm call, the sea knocking at her casket
late for an appointment she had no choice but to

go out as she was, squinting into the mirror
embedded in the sun visor, before the bob, the

undercut the mohican. she would have
walked the strand at tre arddur, waiting for the ferry,

the entertainment industry found
the generation gap an impedance

to maximising the market so the generations mingle
freely, away from the camp fire and the village hall,
down the digital fire wires through the pixellations.

there are many ways to swing a cat and tackle
the problem of implantation
how opposition to imposition can become null

I am a long way from tufts of hair
I cannot display any particular knowledge
the tradition of dancing on graves
is not disrespectful a culture attempts to
repeat itself that's its business

I make records
I keep details, locks of hair

Home on the Range

April 2002

There have been no showers

1.
Leaves not yet
On the tree
Light branches
Between the chest and the elbow
From within tissues
An understanding blanched
In spring pale
Blue water ships
Within the wind

2.

A sprinkling of snow
Tree wisp
What we used to get from transistor radios
Amazed by
How deeply

Bath bed and bored

Hearing the rain listening
To bird song I am without

3.

There are many linkages no I mean languages English
Is an innovation to those who know no better whispering
In the kitchens the border's heavy feet feeling the weight
Of each word, lining it up, and after writing gulping

Like a fish in clover and down the valley walks
My topographical strategies my
Technological drift no collective noun

4.

In my absence something gets through
Beyond the tir that cannot speak
A blood soaked froth upon the loam the
Voiceless whispering its appearance of
Treachery I have chosen the threads of
Many voices as more than an incapacity it
Is dream time and I am overawed or just
Reservation based my high and thin

5.

They flew in the slaughtered for mass burial
Strong words with insufficient force the discourse
Of tanks and heavy artillery a grammar all of its own

I am building your world out of words
I am in protest

It seems like the other side of the world
They seem like minded people
They agree to leave me alone if
Nothing else
Soft days of spring
Maximum recoil
Verbal penetration

6.

Whispering in the kitchen
Keeping their voices down inside

7.

What England expects
Fields full of buttercups
Late oak or early birch
Glacial scarring
Where the criteria are clear
Give up all authority

Lazy poetry or simply
A duck taking off
In series or splashes
Still water
Or small worlds crying
Out ground cover

8.

Day breaks
Prodded by every passing thought
Shell becomes facing poetry a people
You and the poem cracked the bits
That spill out pushed back in and
Day breaks out of sight and mind

9.

In a Welsh context
Or
Nationalism, but not too much of it

Rimbaud a go go
ga ga Armani
da da Derrida
i i English*
ba ba Baudelaire
co co cola
ooh ooh Welsh*

or as summary form (English)

go go
ga ga
da da
eeh eeh
ba ba
co co
ooooh

or in Welsh

go go
ga ga
da da
i i
ba ba
co co
www

**i and w are both vowels in Welsh*
pronounced respectively eeh and ooh

10.

Figure
Like leaning back against the stove
With a slice of cake
And mouthing again all the
Events putting them into
Context a new set of
Characters coming home
Late and sitting down to write
Rather than remembering the event of
Sitting down to write not
What it might be about home
On the range

laid by

1.

The sand lay in loops curves
Around the ripples the sand lay
Whipped wound down
Towards my subject
The pier in sunlight
The chocolate box
The soft centre

A frame around a world
Dry docked
Where the terms are more easily
Defined dick click simplicity
And between sea and sand

2.

A series of relationships like the
Interconnected roads I drive along
That link my past and the receding
Future I drive faster thinking to catch up
But
A slip road takes my eye a young thing
And virtually unused or a worn out
Flyover for shifting cattle then a
Lay by for my tired eyes

3.

A byway with seepage
Tendrils of yellow pollen
Across the tarmac
Water stretched between
Two points then
Allowed to twist

Live pictures
Down my dial up
The air breathed between two mouths
Becoming as dust that falls long held
Domestic habits
A quota never filled

Enough already
No more
The facility for pushing buttons in
Particular sequences as piano playing or
Typing out
Or timed out

The … has cut in the
Banter
Is

4.

A day saying no

Beyond the bridge the walls that
Flowing water makes the
Repairs the cutting back

Ducks walk in the mud
I cried for Kerouac for Jack
I called for Kerouac on a French canal

The village on the right hand side of the road
The left falling away into darkness
Its plainness terrifying

5.

All Over the Place

Along the
mountain line

small rivers

across the other side

to difference and distance
a village with steep sides
where the interference is

behind the waterfall
he drifted his hand in the water
he punched the surface

where do words come from

who does residence
where is health and safety

the cuts are deep

and brain stale

where is the portal and what is the inscription

The Shape I'm In

Body Poem

1.

At the frayed edge of the blanket
below Orion's belt a brake light flickered
between I and the cold night sky in the gap left
between what it might have meant the way things
finally turned a tension I could do without

It has a plan his
forearm shifting independently of the sleeve
fragments leading up the cuff
or off into the veins and capillaries the way the heart is
a stopping off point

Pull into a node in the root system and park up
the hairs magnified to a million times their size
between the sea of light and its illuminations
the syntheses unfold one wave after another
it's time as I imagined all along
spread against the canvas
searching for pure native species
worming its way through the compacted earth

2.

From tree to tumbling
water roars a life without
fading into shadow like

in trying to piece together

a stain in the rug

tufts to the square inch
hugged to a heaving chest
twice its size
out of (shape)
in (condition)

3.

To the south and east a strait
drifting away
down the inner thigh

An inch or two away
the parasite eating the
front of her face her
persona her anti cigarette fat
at the end of a spectacle
drawing in the eidetic denying the
moon hanging in the sky no
cigarette between me no big
deal my face staring back at me
moon hanging in the sky
at the back of the brain

4.

Interference between the wave forms the
slits appended
the dribs and drabs
stuffing the culture
and what is it this
staring into one another's face
we lose ourselves
what the locals have to say
no
way no where

Replay

I stared at the stars until the
sky bled
sandwiches too dry to eat
between work and home
hair down to the bare essentials
hands brown with
a set of assumed positions
held for a while

one hand cleared the water
the other in short chopping strokes
the shape of things to come
and the eyes have it

no single body could be other than
no beginning to end
come compass or the calendar
as the loop rewinds epiphany
becomes commodity oh religious awe replay

what Katy did

its grassy knolls the ridges
where the snow sits
the words gather like
shoals of fish before
darting for the surface

the normal time it takes to meditate
the vicious nature of the Christian faith
clouds slowly clearing off the mountain as
friendly knockings within his frame or
a black art of management
prone
to rushes of blood to the head
when the time came to
question his judgement his
judgement had gone

there are only millions
the vicious nature of practitioners of the Xian faith
could only be expected
messing with the word
attacking the good book
burning the bush
he leant down and bit him the witness said
he shook him like a dog

what Katy did next

The water slapped against the
empty hull full of air the water
sounded against the air underwater a
score that changed again and again

The cat in the sister
no the cat rustling in the back room
no no the cold rustling of feet on the stairs
he stared hard with no mercy in him
the sun setting through the smoke of burning flesh

springing

there is often
something spare such as
a few punctuation marks
sent to the
four corners of the page
to consider their position

leant into the wind
a shed became a cottage
I was warm again
the hedgerows blossomed
across the water oily with cold
a spring bubbles to the surface
the oyster catcher skims
I turned my bicycle into the wind
and rode like the four corners of apocalypse
were firing commas an arrangement
was dissolving before my eyes

there were things
as yet uncovered
grit in the oyster
red in the eye
oh four lidded monster my barrier is broken ah
old man my youth has gone
and the folded came rushing and the brush
easy stuff

not worth a candle

lights

the sun boiled and sputtered
behind the ridge
pools go magenta
the ridges in the sand

and unfolding
within the line's dance
beyond the bright undercurrent
I hear mud rustle
ducks come in to land
tide recedes in intensity

blood filled hands
I mean lands
the duck glides
and lands

anti

I raise my sights to cool air
the bell struck by a single bullet
within the mountain's range

hearing the road
seeing the sun
the cost was too much
no response nobility

no law but order
I pay and pay
the cool of a
summer night

it was a way to travel
that such places might still exist
over swollen feet
and in the silted arteries

hypothetical

that's what I meant
more or less
rustling cicadas or the fire tree
crackling in the wind

we wanders we pays our
dues on the knuckle
there is no local
pricked with a fork

my juices run
I contemplate
he stuck to his guns
down among the rock formations

if that is significant
then take that
it's a mess and the

thunder flies roll in
and then I get greedy
and want to hear it all

turning out the way I am

1.

on the jib of a crane
– Dylan Thomas –
everyone taking their time
as if it was theirs to take
calculating their power of purchase
hanging on by their fingernails
realising at the last minute
and stalking the perimeter of a burnt out building
the last charred spars finally lifting free
hanging in the air
make a window on the world
and how much was that
levered free from its fixings

lining the rooftops or a corridor lined with unidentifiable
left overs out of obscurity and into the main stream
the formal traffic moving smoothly the purpose of spent time
or alongside or even underneath in the culverts
the impact of one world upon another
as in a pit of foam or the overturning of pedestrians

2.

with a border drawn around them the paw marks of a big dog
skidding to a halt in the sand become a vase of flowers!
flocks of terns fluttering into land against a dark hill
onto pale sand over and over the bend of estuary

it is all right like this
you know
I thought something like Laura Ashley would go on forever
well this is an uncertain world but it did seem that way
the dividing line between encircling the contours of the hills
or going native down the valley
is a slipped word in the wrong place
and I can get emotion by repetition I can if all else fails me
or emphasese at the synapse

3.

circling like dogs the gods of war
the lyric eye at the head of the stairs
a sight for sore eyes
the sun breaking the clouds up
everything atrophied in the city
persistently refuse

he constructed his characters with extreme care and then
crumbling into ash in the heat of the moment
conversation at a range of different layers within the wherewithal
four bedrooms, two reception and the usual offices

flying around the place can make for a feeling of self importance
he strolled the garden
his hands clasped behind his back the imaginary coat tails
like an amputated limb
a site for sore eyes lined up like marbles he peered

he was an allusion, a figment of an overwrought imagination
by following in the footsteps of others he caught cold
turned back and began to copy out page upon page
until his genitalia, starved of blood by incessant smoking, shrunk
to a quarter their original size. sure it's a process of rowing back and forth
peering into the still waters and waiting until the cat paws
come rippling across the surface

4.

he tried to annex that which was closest to his skin, the need for income
popping up just below the surface like a bunch of grapes and then
the pale face of a nearest relation coming into view
the hopes and dreams of generations in a world that
endlessly reproduces itself he circled a lost dog preparing to die

the longest journey is straight between the eyes his head
slumped on his chest she shook him gently before
branding him with a route map
of all his misdemeanours. he's no scriptwriter
but can weave a tale when the mood strikes him
and the need is there and traced on the back of his hand
a representation of the London underground as an overlay
across the veins and tendons. I tend towards the
abstract he said picking away at the larger sections

5.

she created the largest nose her face could bear and trimmed her hair back to the
bare necessities it's food I'm really after or at least the smell of it before embarking
on a journey of breast reduction. her ears are already wired, small inserts picking up
the sound of a baby breathing in another's stomach or a dog shitting
on the garden path. every morning the gravel raked until it shines and the plants
which appear randomly scattered take up their allotted places and stand to attention.
she tended them until they became completely dependent, unable to survive
for an even day on their own root system

6.

you are the honeypot to which all things stick
a stranger enters like a virus invading the body of the local
the map unrolls like the waves of the sea
he was operating at the limit of his ability and inclination
in certain company he stood out

he entered the tomb others stood astride leaning into the wind their eyes straining
candle wax spattered the rocks pointing south he controlled himself
at the last minute each molecule easing into the things which came within reach
the world outside skewered by greed her eyes roamed across the map seeking
signs which when I lose my sense of direction he said I'm lost
but with a breath of sea air which hardly touched the sides
yet settled on the stomach wall
I was there and this is how I got there the dam bursts
and all the to sum up as it were outside and inside

7.

far from the coast seagulls whirl against a wall of fog
behind there somewhere the sun
later on the moon low on the horizon and stars hanging
he made a space on the floor surrounded on all sides by piles of junk
old sporting equipment resident with brilliant raw energy
I guess I was fourteen in front of all the guys in front of the poolroom
I couldn't knock her down the stairs outside the church she waited and waited
now that my father had gone back to sea I tried to outlast her my mind and heart
and I wanted to hit her and redeem myself and why didn't I let her know and
everything I say seemed to hurt her more it wasn't my fault my father was at sea
and I was always guilty in the tyranny of the adult world and the door swung shut
there were no names for things what was there to learn and what were the
things I did in the eternity of the walk from the hall to the bathroom
in the grip of a bulldog welded to my arm it was just what it
was all about whatever I did that was so terrible with the people in the street
looking at us a couple of weeks after pearl harbour

8.

within the rhythm of the line the vowels
loop around and catch up with each other
in the company of these people for the very first time
the social circle and the dead centre
the universe moving out and in like a big brute
breathing its intention always uncertain

a metal puzzle
three rings uselessly dangle
terminally interconnected
oh to roll the roads like a hoop
everything turning back on itself
around the roundabouts with no exits
or simply turning the tables, crumbs
the journey into inner space
it's frightening sure and in there the tumblers fall
love grace alienation and psychopathic fear

9.

on the rocks where the sand has shifted a tide mark
out in the bay a new sandbank forms a lagoon
between the beach and the sea
creatures become visible
rainbow anemones, sea mice
fluffing up as they hit the water

he drew on his pipe and blew smoke into the winter air
the two sides of his mind pulling into one as the sea bunched itself
between the beach and the dune
I recall a time when the strait was frozen, or a sandbank formed
at the Southern end the razor shells breathing through
holes in the sand the four points of the compass
and all the flotsam of an Atlantic storm

10.

I begin with a negative and its strap line to the metal shell
from the completed circuit and the brutal logic of forceful repetition
a charge leaks into the churned earth and is discharged

I am up to my knees in it
each generation makes the idle promise
of clarity and coherence the flesh
cut into coordinates a compass
embedded in the navel its needle
reckons due East I pack

and fit my fingers into shapes so familiar that the borders blur
I sit in the corner of an empty house and dream in short bursts whatever
his good intentions scattered in a pile of trash
poking about in the dark cellars of his mind
he came up with death watch beetle, wet rot

on the other hand

shapes emerged which were
down trodden and washed smooth
their origins undetectable

11.

the family portraits were oval and one was a gambling man who
on the refusal of his wife my something grandmother on the father's mother's side
to hand over the takings brought the hammer down and smashed the sideboard
the father moved back in and for no apparent reason lay ill in bed for many years
and when they changed the bedding they would sit him in a chair next to the bed
and cover him with a sheet to save him breathing in the air or something

I am converting you into a thing
I am forming words with the sense of dreams or dreaming
It all depends on uncertainties
Reconciliation between thinking and living or the pure mind
Rising from the daily stew
I can achieve the
All things remain impossible

12.

the casual sideswipe of a car
into the all seeing space my eyes
glued to the windscreen
sometimes it seems easier to think in series
at other times the tune changes of its own volition
maybe only halfway through
oh family life you are both a blessing and a curse
you take many years to come to full fruition
the hand unsteadily carving the Sunday roast
a beaten brow or the gorse bushes
that meander across the garden

after all that effort a pile of ash and the angel swooning
or the fire dragon breathing hard
opacity from all perspectives
war is an intermediate between the tarmac ridges
the sheer drop into subject matter I walk the woods
and a path appears inaccurately as a sequence
illuminating what I know and what I merely

With Reservations

son of heaven the land is – level
inject scientific
politics above orbit
beyond soul the atmosphere

old age on its own never – but oh
whipped by hand and my own
time to myself and high land
the road forks and it's torture

no more a salty acre – as
paradise is slighted
maybe by stature unstable
we narrows we arrow strait

a fashion for glassed eyes – two hands
shift heaven and free earth
the filth crib of his neighbours
splitting gold in her long hair

Manna

lost in hot pools the heather – flowers
folky wordy and fair
bells ring gay in high places
(….) as marsh and honey

to ripeness in the cold dawn – in march
from strange and wishful winter
a weak smile behind the ice flow
its depth beneath the snow plough

still shallow grave impression – bankrupt
          celtic knot ein cwlwm ni
  in celtic not nor bottle
  all directions tout direct

          so busy the sea is
  surface unwinding

counter culture

lit by a thousand complaints – a vision
          of the fool without faith
  nor with he at journey's heart
  in the turns to barren land

out of the night and then in – back in

time has ticked me off kilter – fuck off
            my genetic code sick
   limitations of closure
   first hand second hand reckon

a word to explode syntax – fuck off
            a phrase for every occ
   asion a sentence sentence

right here is site specific – or

a generalisation

almost the last person
a writer wants to find is
a writer between the sheets

dreams of psycho dream night night
if you stick it in don't twist
it is the age of consent

as a bit of a dog tail
inscribed on the backbone or
fixed for performing live or
taking it in from the flanks

Saint Patrick swore in Welsh Mon
Dieu if evidence
don't fit my lord it must be

archaic or out of its time
nominative collapse inward
the names on solid ground and
dated to the death around

eyes deceived repeatedly
by ghost letters grinning past
let play away let ocean drift

or settle as it may and
wind come bathing in the edge
of vagueness where light feathers

In lovelessness I shut my – door
   (love and shut)
The afterglowing sky
   (gain and glow)
Pink cranes in nesting pine
   (pine and nest)
Bamboos with new bloom and I
   (boos and loom)

Sky is lotus in the distance – autumn
   (tus and nut)
Human habitation
   (man and tat)
A crane content beyond clouds
   (con and clown)
Calm limpid evening ripples
   (pid and rip)

White rocks jutting stream see off – all grief
   (rock and reamsee)
Who is it after all
   (ho and of)
Might and morning arm in arm
   (mor and rm)
Cleaning wretch my small entrance
   (etch and ent)

mushroom picking sinecure – sunrise
   (oom and ure)
rows of perfect nipples
   (nip and rip)
dogs bark beyond the border
   (ba and bo)
bow strings hum in the thin wind
   (in and in)

going at dawn to the pa pass – capital
   (aw and ass)
water country tree tops
   (ry and ree)
distant villages emerge
   (ant and ent)
a peculiar dialect
   (ul and al)

distant pacification – skulls
            linked the bumper sticker
   numb for a year the Gobi
   flat out for the boundary

too lazy to write with age – old age
unable to throw off
this heart of mine apart from
habits have come to know me

living without high mountains – bluntly
deep rutted or just stuck
within the brain's waves failing

with all the folded mountains – pleated
complete with just a tuck
the friction of the unstable
or rub down or rough towelling

On the Way

Digging the Road

Because of the hood flapping around her
head in the wind because she could hardly
hear what was being said as if in a crime
scene the camera flashed still morning
under grey skies the scene a broken
toothed death head the open graves lined
up like teeth and at the bottom of every
grave a pale shadow of the past their
skeletons unable to resist absorption
the graves indent the subsoil
and neither the trace of a barrow
above the surface of sweet curves of
alternating material the heads lie east to
watch the coming dawn or the risen Christ
the graves curve as if to accommodate

Beyond the wall the railway the shadow of
the new road already across the empty graves
a line of golden shells set into the tarmac like
cat's eyes the saints surfed around the western
seaboard on Spanish boats filled with clay pots
their fragments carefully resurrected the
definition of an object previously intimate
to domestic fingers is as if precious passed
from hand to hand the boom of tyres along the
expressway a temporary commodity
torn free from its buried past

I return to the map on the computer screen having
sold my right to access no sign of a settlement
reduced to broad outlines layer upon layer and
chasing the cursor we march on through the
landscape free to excess slippage torn
free from her roots lined up for inspection

When two times meet in a single space and
clouds roll in and a storm gathers what language
what pale image of the past pale repetition and alterity
in the throw of policy's dice the shadow of the road

Lines beginning with Road

Openings into spirals of
other words that
arbitrary bit of
land between the fertile
ground and the furrows
on my brow or

Rustling away at dry papers
a series of dates from distant
cultures whose contact is
cuisine numbers 38 and 73 a

Sequence of
points across the
terrain soft
pedestrians flying
off the bumper
sniffing the evening air for
cat within corridors that
link lifeworlds I cannot
imagine and the rain
falls and the dew drops until

Flat and running free a
loose cannon of the past
small pieces of soil
without integrity
roll into the revealed centre
a stone trough for water
or grinding maize and
out from that

There is evidence of giant activity three
toed footprints stone banks brushed aside and
banners strung in parallels as a
guide for those that cannot see the ground

And what is it exactly and alert
as a bird with its head to one side the flexible
framework of its skeleton is a guide
the structures like the language of
defence around the garden and in
the garden and in my heart I tend the
little plants that might one day feed the word

Each object a world
its molecular resistance to
becoming spread its
consistency according to its usage
across the aeons
and the continents the
desiccated bodies or those that
in the acid soil leave only a
trace of carbon or

An object repeatedly used and in
which the shape of another so
impressed is incomplete without
their hand attached and those I
crate up and ship out an unspoken
virus of an idea slams shut

Summer Poem

1.

lilies dead lights flicker each eye moment

or a moonlit sea in time the split oak shuffles

an anthology of clinging vines

2.

a breeze

a mansion with many scented rooms

missing the stream by a whisker
the chance relationship with speech

an order of french
thrown away in the morning

3.

chips off the old block

4.

the perceived disadvantages of the recent past
documented to the last detail

a fine edge to the first word and then the last
and then the one before

fools – diving in the same place over and over
the wreck shifting on the sand and in the tidal race the
molluscs grabbing

5.

(you writes with your heart or you leaves well alone network of veins
surfacing families of mixed blood breaking received wisdom spreading in dark
pools a train of thought with so many carriages and their passengers

6.

spending time

by the pressure of its own weight
one cactus one sick almond anis
bruised underfoot
rice wine horse cheese
geological fruit

crossing and re-crossing from the
centres of production to
those of consumption
breathing out and in across
the city clear bright skin fenced in the things
that never get known soft rolls of
flesh in the pantiles
of my mind and buying the bits and pieces
and spreading them around crouching
against the sun lightening
touching ground
rearranging

after straight time the
penny drops
the underlying form
a collection of points each
lot collecting as a run of water
dried out river beds mixing mud
and blood emptying out the gene pool

the bats come in to land
in the coming dawn the
foul waste of the night tall trees
feathering out dear father the
basis of discipline, distraction
having dreamed of this
the still quiet conscience in the
back of the mountains no
allowances
have to be made
balancing
the inside with the out the
river and its bed each
endlessly changing
each irritating particle

7.

mispronounced places on a map
mouth failing in the turns
bombing the fault lines
as a position from which all
others could open up piles
of discarded ideas a hill
of beans mined and quarried
panned brought to the
surface for inspection

8.

the march of terror
across the overhang
practising low flying
more adagio than arpeggio
certain subterranean rapid moments
lean and brown slivers of broken glass
small pieces of fuselage
propellers devices
for changing direction

9.

natural as water recording its passing the eye to the view rocks projecting short trails of destruction leading nowhere the iron discipline of form each disturbance of the sea bed

10 .

the dying room

abasement garden

his surroundings became him

five blue doors
extending into the air or
the sound of running water
invasion and collection
across the front end
a body of knowledge
eye permanently blinking

horse shit

1.

message arrested it sticks in my mind certain facilities loose
new provision drops steal the parachute silk go
jet ski unpack the pallet life with oil many years without

joss stick smoke in still night against a list of names against the cover
warm certainty of irresistible genetics a newspaper rustles at the appointed hour
a radio clicks on no one picking up
drowning in troubled water his sorrows floating to the surface

we met and talked
he misinterpreted
my body language
an exotic background
is no guide to future performance

he arranged the streets in imitation
he pulled a lever a sign which said stop
an issue of stylistics
rearranging the barriers at the door
the steel cage slowly descending
a range of different holds simulating pain

in the clover fields
a river slowly winds its way across the meadow
his straining fingers for the touch ach
flawed against the deck there are
those whose faces turn up to the sun and
others he stripped the mask
those in the cage and those outside the cage

how much am I located here and what
part of my head is in some place else
the turn   slowly
not ... but

2.

left on the self I sit and think
so many words on the hit list
when the armour comes down
the who clerk who know all now
think shut up think you can too

3.

O spherical moon star music a good
liver sucks your integrity
your gravitational forces

branches that clearly need
trimming - sinister alleys I know
being out of control and spiralling downwards

or the decencies across her bed of descendancies
between the children and twitching their starry eyes
and the sinister alley of horse shit

gas station old macdonalds

Something of the self pulling her down the street her fingers wrapped in his a few hawthorn with wisps of wool clinging and I feel so anxious that this might stop I don't describe the sloe berries.

And this was a place at the head of the lake or just beyond a vantage point the lives they lived without sustaining words but rather stepping out on any morning rain or shine there are always reasons to move.

What are they?

This grove is wild with underwood and broken up and thin grass and kingcups. There's but oh but for old is as. There's no old and for and where a. there's what and her. I cannot escape the deep curve of such loss I would believe I came among these hills.

I come to worship nature people fuck me off. I make the heart that loved her bounded within his chest weak as a lamb foaming like a cataract spring beneath a hill trembling still. Aw Hank you got me now, I take an idea or the crumb of it and cast it upon the water of everything I know. A fish emerges, eats the idea. *That's not what I meant at all I'm not sure how it came out like that.* If there is a normal line then this is it - one or two free associated chemicals drink for those who don't like drink. Better to go down with the ship intact than let the Barbarians aboard. And when someone stands up and says I don't understand thinking they talk for all the little people who don't understand I think go and read some fucking books or look it up when you get home

Part Two

The air went warm to cold then warm again and in the distance lightning flashed it danced across the metal chains. The torrents filled my mouth and then in spouts it ran across my face the laurels bent beneath its weight these things no more their opposite raindrops the size of marbles the time the world could tilt across the curves the sun just cleared the ridge. English is the language of love whispering across the border endlessly finding voice.

That's country for you a place of opposition I sink beneath the scum rising I wash my face. There is no end to it or rather the end is all too soon. Hedgerows ripped away before my eyes the brew a wasteful place of little yield, hard to turn and slow to grow. Where small animals scutter, where mapping merely means the big guns wear wellingtons. The sink is now a trough the bed head a hurdle the compost heap a warm place for slow worms.

Being contrary he accumulated companies with no final analysis no real growth potential no obvious market no track record. He took the science out of financial speculation and replaced it with juxtaposition.

Afterword

Most experience no longer takes place in the place in which it is located. If anything links these poems it is an exploration of the difficulty of simultaneously existing in a number of different locations from a number of different perspectives. The poems seem to explore potentially contradictory positions; between wanting to stay and wanting to get away, between celebrating and despising the local and between welcoming and resenting intrusion.

The title tries to link the body to the landscape and the way in which we read off the scale of our surroundings via the body. The 'stretch' is of land or water; it is the extension of the body and it is a stretch of time.

This book is in six parts. The divisions are porous and the parts bleed into each other. The poems were written using a variety of procedures; from a daily journal, from logs of specific journeys, from following the progress of a road being built, from archaeological digs, from the experience of a body in space, from translation across time and place and through the use of particular forms. Some are located in specific places; most move between places and some remain in between.

As I re-read these poems there may be too much landscape. Living in north Wales between the mountains and the sea that's hard to avoid. But I do seem to have tried to detail the way a local inter-relates with the global, how locales and locals can talk to each other and how speech and writing might jump from place to place and terminal to terminal.

Ian Davidson
December, 2003

www.ingramcontent.com/pod-product-compliance
Lightning Source LLC
Chambersburg PA
CBHW032056150426
43194CB00006B/550
* 9 7 8 0 9 0 7 5 6 2 4 4 3 *